LESSONS FROM THE PAST: FAMOUS ARCHAEOLOGISTS, ARTIFACTS AND RUINS

World Geography Book | Social Studies Grade 5 | Children's Geography & Cultures Books

First Edition, 2020

Published in the United States by Speedy Publishing LLC, 40 E Main Street, Newark, Delaware 19711 USA.

© 2020 Baby Professor Books, an imprint of Speedy Publishing LLC

Baby Professor Books are available at special discounts when purchased in bulk for industrial and sales-promotional use. For details contact our Special Sales Team at Speedy Publishing LLC, 40 E Main Street, Newark, Delaware 19711 USA. Telephone (888) 248-4521 Fax: (210) 519-4043.

10 9 8 7 6 * 5 4 3 2 1

Print Edition: 9781541949959
Digital Edition: 9781541951754
Hardcover Edition: 9781541976184

See the world in pictures. Build your knowledge in style.
www.speedypublishing.com

TABLE OF CONTENTS

What Do Archaeologists Do? 9

Famous Archaeological Finds. 15

Human Remains:Lucy 19

Human Remains: The Peking Man 23

Lost Civilizations: Pompeii. 27

Lost Civilizations: Machu Picchu 31

Lost Civilizations: Gobekli Tepe 37

Ancient Artifacts: The Rosetta Stone. 41

Ancient Artifacts: Dead Sea Scrolls 45

Ancient Artifacts: The Terracotta Warriors 49

Ancient Treasures: King Tut. 53

Ancient Treasures: Venus de Milo. 57

Ancient Treasures: Hoxne Hoard 61

Famous Archaeologists: The Leakeys 65

Famous Archaeologists: Howard Carter 69

Summary 72

ARTIFACTS AND A BODY CAST FROM THE ROMAN RUINS AT POMPEII NEAR NAPLES AND MT. VESUVIUS, CAMPANIA, ITALY.

Studying the past can help us learn about the people, places, and cultures that came before us and shaped our world. Archaeologists are special kinds of scientists who examine the things that people in the past left behind. That could mean places, like ancient ruins or buried cities, artifacts[1], like pottery, tools, or artwork, or human remains, such as fossils and mummies.

[1] Artifact – An object made by humans.

Although movies often make archaeology seem like an exciting and glamorous job, it is rare that archaeologists unearth actual hidden treasure, but what they have found is nonetheless important. Still, there have been some exciting and important archaeological discoveries made over the years. In this book, we will look at what an archaeologist does. We will also introduce some famous archaeologists, significant artifacts, and important ruins. Let's get started.

ARCHAEOLOGISTS WORKING ON A DIG SITE
AT CHEDWORTH ROMAN VILLA, UK

WHAT DO ARCHAEOLOGISTS DO?

ARCHAEOLOGISTS MUST LEARN ABOUT HISTORY, CULTURE, ARCHITECTURE, LANGUAGE, AND HUMAN EVOLUTION.

Archaeologists must learn about history, culture, architecture, language, and human evolution. They must also know about chemistry, historic research, and human behavior. Archaeologists use the information they learn to make educated guesses as to where ancient settlements or historic artifacts may be.

Archaeologists also do field work. They travel to dig sites and do the dirty work of looking for artifacts that have been buried in the ground for hundreds, maybe even thousands, of years. The work can often be tedious. The scientists use small chisels and brushes to slowly and carefully remove dirt and debris for tiny fragments of bone, pottery, or other artifacts. They analyze the objects they find and draw conclusions based on when they have found and how those fit in with previously known information.

AN ARCHAEOLOGIST CAREFULLY
DIGGING OUT HUMAN REMAINS.

FAMOUS ARCHAEOLOGICAL FINDS

Some places and artifacts from ancient times have always been known, such as the Great Pyramid of Giza, Stonehenge, and the Colosseum. Other places and objects were lost to time and rediscovered much later. In the next section, we will discuss some of the most famous and important archaeological discoveries of all time. These include human remains, lost civilizations, and ancient artifacts. Each one of these discoveries helped further our understanding of our long-ago past.

GREAT PYRAMIDS OF GIZA IN CAIRO, EGYPT

STONEHENGE IN WILTSHIRE, ENGLAND

COLOSSEUM IN ROME, ITALY

HUMAN REMAINS: LUCY

n 1974, a team of archaeologists, including the British Mary Leakey, the French Yves Coppens, and the American Donald Johnson, were excavating in a region of Ethiopia looking for evidence of early human origins.

MARY LEAKEY

YVES COPPENS

DONALD JOHNSON

They discovered the shin bone of a previously unknown ancestor of human beings, which led them to unearth a partial skeleton of Australopithecus afarensis, or Lucy, an early hominin species. Lucy dates back more than 3.2 million years and demonstrates an evolutionary step in human development, walking upright.

THE REMAINS OF ONE OF THE EARLIEST HUMAN ANCESTORS, LUCY, ON DISPLAY WITHIN THE NATIONAL MUSEUM OF ETHIOPIA, ADDIS ABABA, ETHIOPIA.

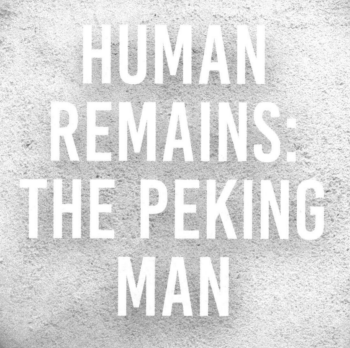

HUMAN REMAINS: THE PEKING MAN

PEKING UNION
MEDICAL COLLEGE IN
BEIJING, CHINA

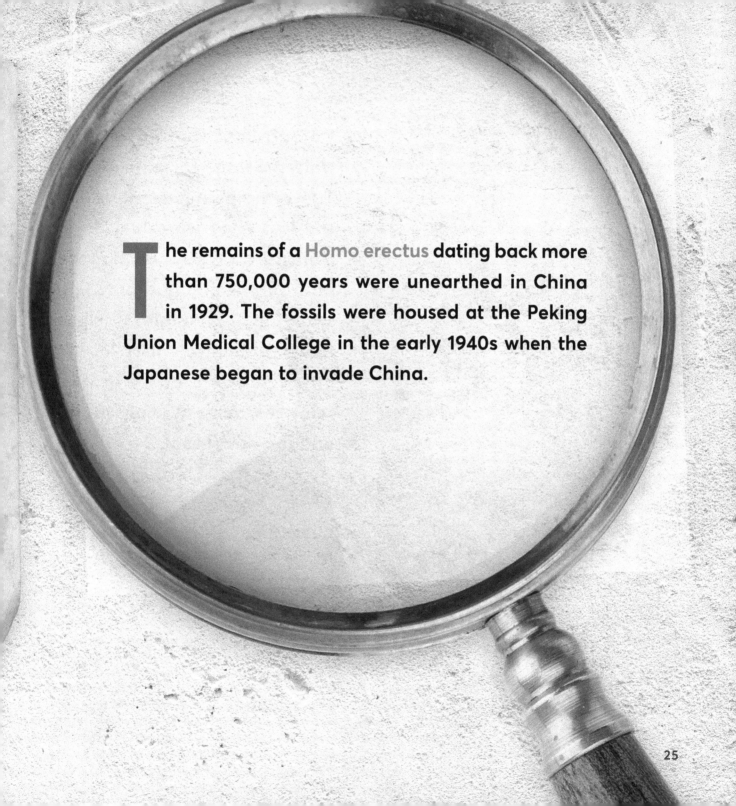

The remains of a Homo erectus dating back more than 750,000 years were unearthed in China in 1929. The fossils were housed at the Peking Union Medical College in the early 1940s when the Japanese began to invade China.

The fossils of the Peking Man were packaged up and sent to the United States for safekeeping. The remains never made it to the US. They were lost during transport. One tooth, however, had been smuggled out. From studying this single fossilized tooth, paleontologists learned much about early human relatives, such as diet, speech, and the use of tools.

LOST CIVILIZATIONS: POMPEII

The eruption of Mount Vesuvius in 79 AD caused the widespread destruction of the city of Pompeii. Residents of the city were killed by poisonous gas and buried under ash and pumice, where they remained for centuries.

RUINS OF POMPEII OVERLOOKING MOUNT VESUVIUS IN THE DISTANCE, CAMPANIA, ITALY.

In 1748, workers uncovered the ancient city, which had been almost perfectly preserved under the rubble. Mysteriously, there were strange voids found all over the ancient ruins. To the astonishment of archeologists, it was discovered that these voids formed when the ash surrounded a person and that person's remains decomposed over time. By pouring plaster into the voids, the scientists could create eerie molds of the Pompeii victims, showing the citizens in their final moments of life.

OLDS OF THE POMPEII
ICTIMS, SHOWING THE
IZENS IN THEIR FINAL
MOMENTS OF LIFE.

Since the tragedy happened so quickly, researchers have been able to use the finds at Pompeii – the food left on tables, the art in progress, the work tools, and more – to learn about everyday life in the Roman city.

REMAINS OF A HOME INTERIOR IN POMPEII FROM THE ROMAN EMPIRE PERIOD BURIED IN THE ERUPTION OF MOUNT VESUVIUS.

High in the Andes Mountains in southern Peru sit the 15th century Incan city of Machu Picchu, also called the "Lost City of the Incas".

MACHU PICCHU, CUSCO, PERU

Historians theorize that the ancient city was built as a home for Pachacuti, an Incan emperor. It appears, however, that the city was abandoned during the Spanish conquest, about a century after it was built.

PACHACUTI

To say Machu Picchu was a lost city is a bit misleading. Local people living in the area always knew about the ruined city, but it became internationally known after it was rediscovered by an explorer and historian named Hiram Bingham in 1911.

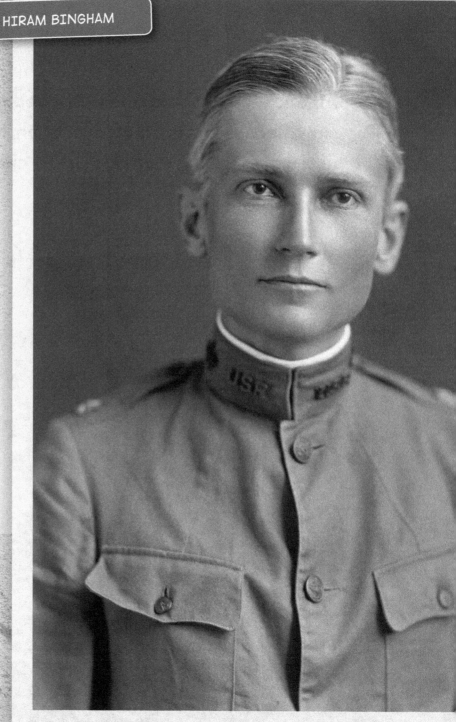

Machu Picchu is significant because the ruins were intact and had not been plundered. When the Spanish invaded South America, they looted and destroyed nearly all ancient Incan sites. Because of its isolated location, Machu Picchu remained untouched, giving archeologists a chance to study the ruins.

TEMPLE OF THE CONDOR IN MACHU PICCHU

LOST CIVILIZATIONS: GOBEKLI TEPE

Ancient ruins discovered in Turkey in 1994 by Klaus Schmidt of the German Archaeological Institute turned out to be one of the oldest known megaliths[2].

KLAUS SCHMIDT

[2]   Megalith – A stone of great size used in ancient construction.

The site has been dated to be between the 10th and 8th millennium BC...a time when historians thought humans lived only in hunter-gatherer communities and had not yet erected permanent cities.

GOBEKLI TEPE ARCHAEOLOGICAL SITE
NEAR SANLIURFA (URFA), TURKEY

The discoveries made by the researchers studying Gobekli Tepe are significant because they rewrite the timeline of human progression.

STELAE AT GOBEKLI TEPE EXCAVATION SITE

ANCIENT ARTIFACTS: THE ROSETTA STONE

Archaeologists had long been fascinated with ancient Egyptian sites. There, they encountered drawings and symbols on tombs and temples, they believed, represented a written language. But all attempts to decipher the symbols, or hieroglyphics[3], failed.

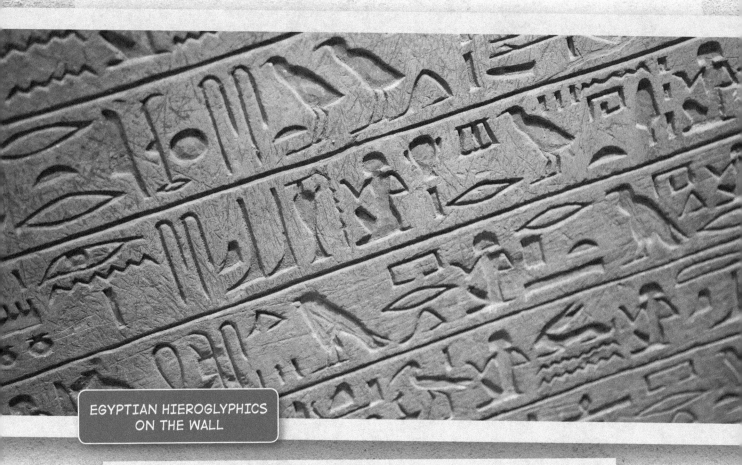

EGYPTIAN HIEROGLYPHICS
ON THE WALL

[3]   Hieroglyphics – Written language using a system of pictures or recognizable symbols.

That is, until French soldiers were sent to Egypt by Napoleon Bonaparte from 1798 to 1801. A group of them unearthed a large stone slab – that we now call the Rosetta Stone – in July of 1799 in the Nile Delta. On this stone, was an official government decree written in three languages…ancient Greek, Demotic, and Egyptian hieroglyphics.

NAPOLEON BONAPARTE

The Rosetta Stone, which is now on display at a museum in England, was the key to deciphering the written language of the Egyptians.

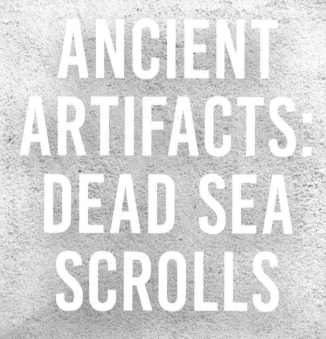

ANCIENT ARTIFACTS: DEAD SEA SCROLLS

A shepherd searching for a lost goat in 1946 in the Judaean Desert made an incredible discovery. Hidden inside a cave near the Dead Sea were numerous clay jars with ancient scrolls that were some of the oldest surviving manuscripts of the Hebrew bible.

QUMRAN CAVE 4, ONE OF THE CAVES IN WHICH THE SCROLLS WERE FOUND AT THE RUINS OF KHIRBET QUMRAN IN THE DESERT OF ISRAEL.

Scholars and historians are still studying the manuscripts of the Dead Sea Scrolls, which have proven to be a tremendous source of information about ancient linguistics, history, and religion.

FRAGMENT OF THE DEAD SEA SCROLLS ON DISPLAY AT THE QUMRAN CAVES NATIONAL PARK IN ISRAEL

ANCIENT ARTIFACTS: THE TERRACOTTA WARRIORS

A group of farmers digging a well in rural China in 1974 unearthed a collection of terracotta[4] shards and fragments. When Chinese archaeologists were brought to excavate[5] the site, they soon realized that they found the fabled tomb of Qin Shi Huang, the first Emperor of China.

QIN SHI HUANG

4   Terracotta – Reddish-brown fired clay.
5   Excavate – To expose by digging.

Dating back to about 210 BC, the tomb was surrounded by an army of more than 8,000 unique statues of warriors crafted out of terracotta. Each figure has different facial features, clothing, and gestures. The site is still being excavated today and more finds are being discovered.

MUSEUM OF THE TERRACOTTA WARRIORS, MAUSOLEUM OF THE FIRST QIN EMPEROR, XIAN, SHAANXI PROVINCE, CHINA

ANCIENT
TREASURES:
KING TUT

One of the greatest archaeological finds of all time was the discovery of the tomb of King Tutankhamun in Egypt's Valley of the Kings.

VALLEY OF THE KINGS IN EGYPT

A British explorer named Howard Carter had long suspected that there was an undiscovered tomb in the Valley and he used his research and knowledge of previously discovered tombs to pinpoint where he thought a tomb may be. On November 4, 1922, Carter located the entrance to the tomb.

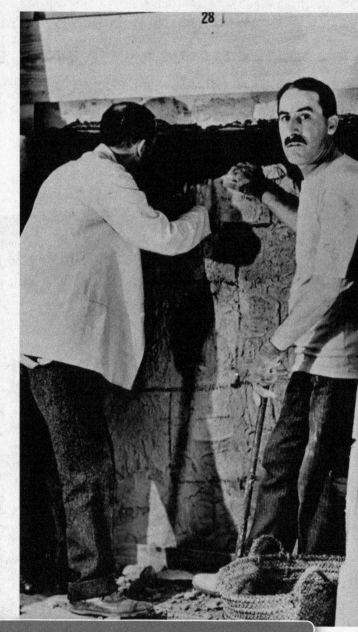

HOWARD CARTER AT THE ENTRANCE TO KING TUT'S TOMB IN THE VALLEY OF THE KINGS, EGYPT

Inside, was an undisturbed tomb of an Egyptian pharaoh that had not been raided by tomb robbers. The treasures that were discovered in the tomb – gold, jewels, and other priceless artifacts – provided a trove of information for Egyptologists[6] and historians and helped to advance the understanding of ancient Egypt.

AN OVERHEAD SHOT OF KING TUT'S TOMB

6   Egyptologist – A scientist who studies Egyptian antiquities.

ANCIENT TREASURES: VENUS DE MILO

The Venus de Milo, the armless marble statue, is one of the most recognizable ancient statues in the world today and is a symbol of beauty and grace.

VENUS DE MILO STATUE AT LOUVRE MUSEUM, PARIS. FRANCE

The stunning, yet damaged statue was discovered buried in the ground on the island of Milos in the Aegean Sea in 1820 by a peasant digging in the ground. Historians believe that the classic statue was made between 130 and 100 BC and may have depicted the Greek goddess of beauty and love, Aphrodite.

A PLAQUE INDICATING THE POSITION OF THE VENUS DE MILO FIND, NEAR TRIPITI, MILOS, GREECE

The Venus de Milo has become famous around the world because it captures the timeless artistry of ancient Greece. It is currently housed at the Louvre Museum in Paris.

THE LOUVRE MUSEUM IN PARIS, FRANCE

ANCIENT TREASURES: HOXNE HOARD

n November of 1992, a farmer in England lost his hammer in a field. He called his friend to come over with his metal detector to help him find it. In addition to the lost hammer, the two friends discovered the Hoxne Hoard, an oak box or chest filled with gold and silver coins, jewelry, and precious artifacts dating back to the 4th century.

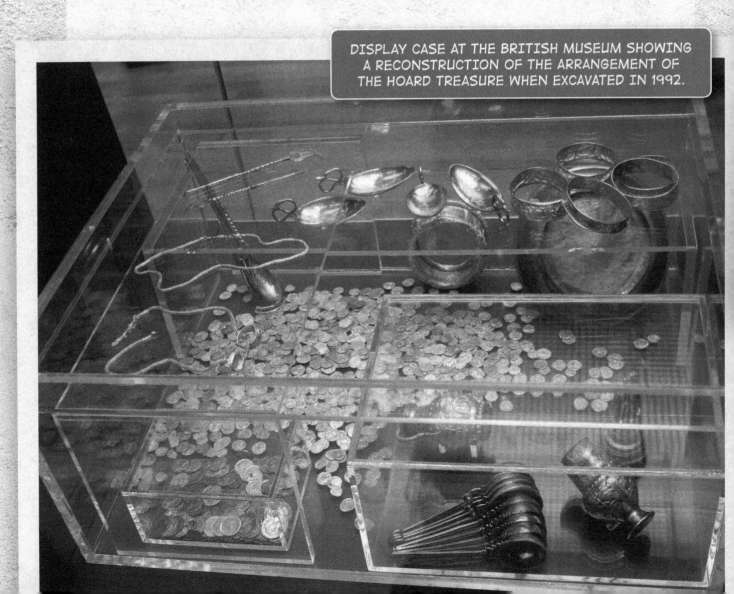

DISPLAY CASE AT THE BRITISH MUSEUM SHOWING A RECONSTRUCTION OF THE ARRANGEMENT OF THE HOARD TREASURE WHEN EXCAVATED IN 1992.

The items were all Roman in origin, so it was speculated that the treasure was buried to keep it safe during the Roman occupation of Britain. The Hoxne Hoard included many rare and unusual items that gave historians and archaeologists valuable insight into the era.

HOXNE HOARD PEPPER POTS

COINS FROM THE HOXNE HOARD

HOXNE HOARD GOLD BODY CHAIN

FAMOUS ARCHAEOLOGISTS: THE LEAKEYS

Louis and Mary Leakey and their children, most notably their son Richard and his wife Maeve, made tremendously significant finds while excavating in Africa's Olduvai Gorge.

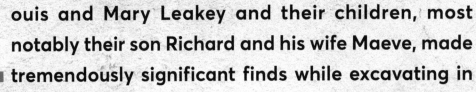
LOUIS AND MARY AT OLDUVAI GORGE

LOUIS AND MARY LEAKEY

RICHARD LEAKEY

While searching for evidence of human origins, they unearthed fossil remains of early hominids, stone age tools, and even a set of prehistoric footprints that were preserved in mud that shows a primate walking on two legs. The work of the Leakey family has proven invaluable to our understanding of pre-humans.

MARY AND LOUIS LEAKEY STUDYING SKULL FRAGMENTS

FAMOUS ARCHAEOLOGISTS: HOWARD CARTER

Perhaps the best-known archaeologist is Howard Carter, the person who discovered King Tut's tomb. A British explorer, archaeologist, and Egyptologist, Carter helped to revolutionize the way that archaeological sites were preserved, documented, and excavated.

HOWARD CARTER

He also combined historical research and geography to make educated guesses about the locations of important ancient sites. Howard Carter's work helped to increase our understanding of Egypt's ancient cultures.

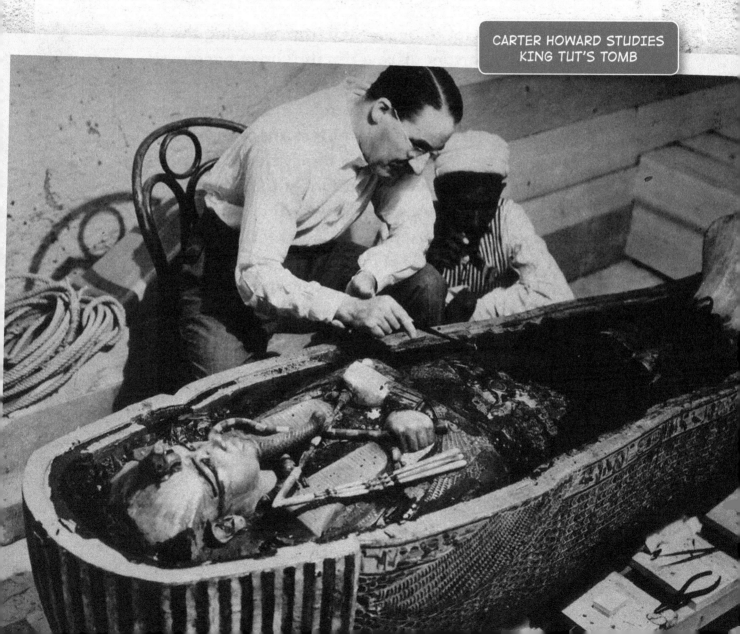

CARTER HOWARD STUDIES KING TUT'S TOMB

SUMMARY

There is a lot to be learned from studying the past. The important discoveries that have been made – including ancient artifacts and lost civilizations – provide us with valuable information to help us unravel the secrets of the past. From the remains of early humans, we can better understand our family tree. By examining ancient treasures, we gain insight into what was sacred and valuable to ancient peoples. And from old stone carvings and manuscripts, we can read the messages that were written by people long ago. The work that is done by archaeologists, paleontologists, and other researchers all provide vital lessons of the past.